Love in Interesting Times

Wyatt Underwood

Lulu Press

ISBN 978-1-105-54945-8

To all the women who have taught me about love. To all the people who have helped me see our interesting times.

Table of Contents

introduction

Love is. Some people think they can define or describe it. I celebrate it, coming, staying, and going. I prefer staying.

A friend writes love poems that fascinate me: they are so unromantic! Mine are mostly romantic, but sometimes shaded with wryness or rue at the forms love takes in our times.

And we do live in interesting times. I thank the Chinese for the saying, blessing or curse, which keeps me aware of that. Our times are interesting not only for all that's happening in them, but for what we do with those events, for the lies we tell ourselves, and the lies we live by.

May you enjoy these poems, and may you enjoy our interesting times.

Love

bond

"I dropped the soap into warm water"
my friend said
"it damned near dissolved"
he grinned
"I told my wife it was like me
in her love
I not only turn soft, I damned near
disappear"
I grinned at him but thought of us
how differently
we experience our loving each other
as if two metals bond
but keep their separateness
except somehow
each stronger than when alone

distinctions

you drive, and I, watching, smile
partly because you drive
like I'd like to think I would
if I drove
but mainly admiration
such patience, skill, and attention
so seldom a bad word
for other drivers' lack
it is a job, you get it done
with nothing personal involved
and when we get there
you smile at me
with everything personal involved
what useful distinctions!

Petals

I do not buy you candy
and seldom flowers
but I do write you poems
that celebrate you
and celebrate our love
and sometimes to remind me
or to tease
you tear the petals off them
as if deciding whether I meant them
but when you do
you're careful to preserve
the words and lines intact
showing, I suspect,
you really know
and really know I love you
it's true
I do

craziness

I ride home in the rain
not the short ride from work
but back from a farther visit
on which I'd gambled for good weather
and lost my bet
but still arrive at home all smiles
drenched and soggy but abeam
you laugh and bring me
a bucket for my clothes
tell me to shower warm
so you can hug me soon
and later listen while I try to tell
how riding in the rain can be such fun
you shake your head and allow
my craziness it's play
knowing that I also
am crazy over you

promise and report

how could we have known
so many years ago
that we'd still say now
"I love you" and so mean it?
we couldn't, of course
so some would say we gambled
but I would say we didn't
we grinned and said "I love you"
as a promise as well as a report
and kept that promise every day
each hour and every minute
and still do, still grinning
some promises are wonderful to keep

shopping

you walk up in a store
"shopping for me?" you tease
you know I wasn't
but I'm quicker than that
"please help," I ask
you laugh
and list half a dozen items
I would've thought of none of them
but we walk from the store
and you carry all of them
as if each one said "I love you"

faux Atlas

this week my mood has swung
from grim to glum and back
with an occasional break into laugh
you help, you tease, you joke
and slowly clouds burn away
I can't even say what brought them in
just that they piled up all around
and weighed as if I had
changed places with Atlas
I doubt he noticed
but thank you sweet woman
for being the steady sun
and flickering wind
and reminding me again we love

let's marry

you didn't have to stop, but you did
you didn't have to smile, but you did
you didn't have to kiss, but you did
what had we left to do? "let's marry"
I said and you said "sure"
it wasn't quite that simple
but some were sure it was
and some of them predicted
dire consequences from such foolishness
yet here we are nearly thirty years later
still grinning at statistics
still filling days with kisses
and some say now it is a foolish way
for us to pass our days
but still, you walk into a room
I smile, and you smile back
and we live happily so far
so here am I, love's fool and maybe life's
love's fool and maybe life's

understand

I never understand, you are yourself
and every woman I have ever known
women I have never known and never could
you are mystery and romance and allure
you are blessing and kindness and aloof
you are, you are, you are, and I am glad
glad to love you and be loved by you
and even if mind never understands
body is satisfied with glad
spirit with reverence
and heart with love

how might

how might I love thee
loved I not the mountains, desert, and sea?
I do not know, nor am I likely now to learn
but love I you as I love you
sometimes like wind drops down the mountain's lee
sometimes like sandstorms prowl the desert's skin
sometimes like waves ripple the surface of the sea
and sometimes like moonlight bathes all three
but doubt you not, so long as mountains, deserts, and seas
can take the breath and heart of me
so long and longer I love thee

and this I you

here we are, packing again
we've done it, what, a dozen times?
counting our honeymoon?
this time we're heading to the mountains
to spend a night or two in comfort
and with friends we've made
who might have remained
host and hostess, fellow poets,
or just people we smile and nod to
I watch you checking items on your list
my computers, yours, items of clothing
a gallon of coffee we can microwave
before the world is quite ready
for humans to be up
you look at me and smile
"won't you need extra socks?"
I grin and get them
you know you can count on me
packing the electronics we might need
usually even the chargers for them
but I'd forget my sweater or my scarf
until we got there
preventing that is just one of the ways
you love me. and this I you

wind

Outside, the wind
prowls the trees,
tests shutters, and
knocks over cans.
"I wait," it says,
or so I hear.
Inside, I make
more coffee and
cinnamon toast.
Defy the wind.
You know and watch,
smile at my ways,
smile at me, and
rekindle love.
I stand and breathe,
caught again in
what fills a chest,
what clears a mind.
I take your hand.
The wind can wait.

Interesting Times

working man

Before I learned we had a server down
and I had to ride in to start it up again,
while the morning was still cool and dark
and only the drunk downstairs giggled and laughed
and carried half a conversation on
with someone I could not see nor hear
perhaps his bottle, I was thinking of that lad,
me at eighteen, who put me on this path.
He must have been brighter than he seems now sometimes.
For instance, he seethed but waited the three years
before he left home. Yes, at fifteen he had decided
but two acquaintances left and were brought home.
He didn't need that, so he stayed, pretended patience,
and escaped when it was legal, and probably just as well.
What would he have done? He didn't know yet about rent
or groceries or shelter. Work, yes.
He'd had a job since twelve,
enough to buy himself shirts and boots,
had paid for his Lambretta and a gun.
I think he thought he could walk out
and start work as a cowboy, or forest ranger.
Yeah, those would have been fun jobs!
He probably had no idea where to look for them
but may have suspected they were hard to find.
At fifteen. Billy the Kid had, and young Buffalo Bill,
but the west had been wilder in their day

And labor cheap as life. It was the fifties when the lad looked.

Men still owned their wives and children, pretty much.

And despite Ayn Rand's promise, everything required permission.

She said the lefties made that so,

the same bad people who agreed that laborers should get paid,

and work only forty hours, and be older than twelve.

It looked a lot to that seething lad like parents, teachers, and bosses

had more to do with his needing all those permissions

than people who voted for a minimum wage,

against which he wasn't quite sure why he should protest

since bosses would have been happy to pay

a quarter an hour or a day, like an allowance

without the room and board. Room & board! Maybe that's

why cowboying and rangering looked so good!

That and escape from the city where everything he did

was someone else's business. If children were the city's garden,

then every flower had a committee of gardeners

who didn't necessarily agree, but knew the flower

needed correcting, needed binding to a stake

so it could grow strong and free.

He thought they meant safe, and could barely wait to escape.

And eighteen came and off he went, out to the desert,

White Sands Missile Range, to apprentice as a techie.

He learned what school could never teach him.

respect for working men and respect from them.

Work? He helped dig a trench and lay a cable in it

that connected at one end to a trailer full of electronics

and at the other to a repeater, that strengthened signals and relayed them.

He maintained cameras that took twelve-hundred frames a minute.

He maintained electronics that captured doppler and telemetry.

He helped build one of those trailers full of electronics.

He built antennas, helped test and document them.

And graduated magna cum laude with more than a degree,

experience in making things and making them work.

And fifty years later, I'm still doing that,

still keeping things working when they want to quit.

And from this reverie an alarm called, a program that I wrote

tells me a server's not responding, not doing its job.

I wince, then grin, my work calls me to work.

And off I ride to make what I built work again,

with any luck, before its users have reason to complain.

It is a life, I smile as I ride, not cowboying nor rangering

but satisfyingly like both, keeping things going

that on their own might die or become useless.

It's what a man does, I think, a working man.

boys and men

boys
I was one
sitting near a group of of them
I remember
and am surprised too
what curious beings!
what they want most
certainly what I most wanted
and it sounds like
each of them wants too
a girl who thinks he is it
but the only way each knows
is to outboy the others
burp, belch, fart, scratch
holler, make fun, boast
this is how to win a girl?
it was
it sounds like it still is
well, probably it's good training
what a girl first has to learn
is lowered expectations
no prince available
not even a frog with a crown
burp, belch, fart, scratch
holler, make fun, boast
hell, even hit her in the arm
translates to please love me
even for a minute or two
what curious beings!

how do they ever become us?
oh dear! are we still them?
what curious beings!
boys and men

live and let live

live and let live
wise governments survive by that, I think
what you and I do to our wives, children, and friends
most governments leave alone
as they do what we do for our loved ones
once or so a year the government taxes us
but only so much that a month of complaining works
we're satisfied and get back to what really interests
and for most of the year they parade and posture
entertaining and irritating us but harmlessly
we prate and grouse and grumble
but neither they nor we have much interest
in doing much about the other
it's only when they panic
or when some rabble-rouser really works his magic
that we rise and raise voices and fists
and they must send the soldiers in
to remind us of our place
and soon we are all happy once again
they put on their show and we complain
and the world works as it must
and on some anniversary
they give us fireworks
live and let live

reassurance

I listen to people talk
and hear a world I've never known
children are safe, and women
men work hard and are appreciated
even promoted, or find happier jobs
savings grow and do not melt away
I suppose if I listened a little harder
the sun would always shine, or moon
except for regularly scheduled rains
I do not know this world
in mine you can't trust priests with kids
and every man is the potential
for rape or death or maiming
well, nearly every man
a few seem the potential
only for caution
but I don't trust them much
and so I welcome overhearing
two mothers agree as an elevator drops
that they must leave early every day
they dare not let their children walk alone

advice

it was two-thirty in the afternoon
no one should be in a bar then
even the jukebox knows it's wrong
refuses to play except happy songs
and no one there wants to hear those
I was there, and seven others
no one with anyone else
the bartender watched us warily
or maybe I only thought he did
one of us smoked, or smoke drifted
from the cigarette in his hand
I never saw him take a drag
his cigarette stayed the same length
or so I thought, not measured
the woman at the bar sighed
turned around, surveyed the room
then stood and slinked to my table
sat down and asked, "buy me a shot?"
I grinned and signaled the bartender
he brought her a shot and traded me
a full beer for my almost empty
"what you in for?" she asked
I grinned again, "apathy, I guess,
stopped for a beer and haven't found
interest enough in anything
to walk me out of here"
she nodded soberly and drank her shot
then signaled for another
"be careful with that," she opined

"four of the others did that
I think in ninety-seven, two haven't moved
in so long Jake doesn't know whether to call
the coroner, they don't even decay"
she smiled, at me, her story, her new shot
I couldn't tell, then she looked wry
"why am I talking about them?
every Tuesday afternoon I sit in here
get someone new to buy me shots
haven't had sex this decade
don't even know if it still works
have you heard?" I laughed uneasily
"it did last month," I claimed
she nodded, "good to know
take my advice, you swim? then find
a beach and swim out far as ocean lets you
if she returns you to the shore
find somewhere else to drink"
I did, I did, I did

the city continued

"I got a gun"
the boy
on the other end
of the bus bench
said
"good," I said
"you know how
to use it?"
he stared at me
"on whom?
and when?"
"you're crazy!"
he said
and fled

homework

it was homework, see?
find an image
have it tell somethin' about your life
goddam
so I read Creeley and H.D.
like she told me
the teacher did
and still couldn't think of nuthin
then on my way to school
there it was
in the alley
a broken toilet
leaned against the dumpster
draining

world history as I learned it in the United States

in the beginning was Greece
so we could have democracy
then there was Rome
so we would know law'n'order
and empire, oh, and peace
then everybody traveled out of Asia
to collide in Spain
or float to Africa by accident
then there was England
and God saw that the world was good
men had almost learned their lessons
ah! but then came the United States
and God saw that all was very good
He didn't need to pay attention any more
men were as good as they could get
and God went on sabbatical
and left fixing the world to us

vigil

he stared across the desert
not that he could see anything in the dark
not really
he remembered the shapes of rolls and swells
and thought the varying darknesses agreed with those
those memories anyway
and somewhere out there was a horizon
it cut off the star patterns he supposed
he prob'ly should be able to figure out that
if there were a moon, yes, and if he'd chosen other work
he took another swig from his canteen
tried harder to see in the dark
but saw instead only the kid
sneering as he'd strapped him into the chair
"lookit'm," the kid derided, "as if for a circus,
only some of them see a circus of sympathy
what for? I didn't ask for their feelings
any more'n I asked for them
how do they get tickets? is there a lottery?"
the kid had leaned back for the cap
said something that it muffled
then jerked and twitched and smoked
when the warden gave the signal
the warden hadn't watched, of course
given the signal and looked away
the doctor had come in to check for signs of life
none, of course, he did his job well
and after some of them he came out here and waited
he wasn't sure for what

imagination fails

I listen to my friend talk about humans
and recognize she describes no one I know
men I know are poised to rage, to fight
hers to discuss, to work together
women she knows are more reasonable men
mine like no man I ever met, ready to love
to disdain, to go their own way more likely than mine
alone, with each other, or with me if I will
her people could live in peace
mine might ignore each other a while
might fight together if attacked
but are as likely to demand "that's mine"
even if they added "but you can use it"
her men greet when they meet
mine loosen guns in holsters
before they're close enough to speak
her men might assemble to work together
mine are born into groups ready to bite
subdue and enslave, but can work together
briefly, if they need or must
her people think and act
mine prickle and react
but can suppress both long enough
to build a house or bridge
she thinks I misunderstand my people
but I live among them
I have dodged their clubs, knives, and teeth
and have laid track with them
I wish her people well and hope they exist

but suspect that if they do
my people will make hers slaves

slipping it in

reverence
I haven't much to give
and what I have I reserve
for women and the written word
and not all written words at that
they pretty much have to make my kind of sense
and probably to agree with me
although I have been known to read and learn
but seldom from someone who flails around
at grammar or at spelling
and almost never from someone
who disrespects the working men and women
or thinks democracy means government
of, by, and for the wealthy
it is, like any other,
but I like to believe democracy
is for the rest of us, knowing it a lie
what good is faith if it fails lies that comfort?
and so I cherish that at least in part
and sometimes law-makers protect us
from themselves and other oppressors
and reverence skeptically
thinkers who write the same or nearly
and scorn those who claim truth as excuse
to lick the ass that shits them
oh wait! I can't say that!
please find the polite way to say it
and slip it in where my words offend
and know at the same time

that polite and proper legislators
slip it into your freedoms
and maybe you

truth

we don't lie
do we?
I mean, not really
we just get caught sometimes
with having said what we can't deny
whose meaning facts won't justify
it was an accident
and besides
you didn't understand what I really meant
I was interrupted
before I finished
if I had been allowed to finish
I could have weaseled, hedged, and modified
beyond your having any clue
what I might mean
and so
it was no lie
simple misunderstanding
and your fault besides
see?

Waking

waking, my mind balks
it doesn't so much like
the rules that warp
and bend in dreamtime
but neither does it
so much like the rules
that seemingly hold
steady in what we call
reality, which
confused Plato til
he thought he
lived in a cave
and spoke to shadows
that toyed with his
reality which I
pray I will never know
despite my being no
praying man but
still, waking, my mind
balks at so many rules
it does not know and
cannot

horror

puppy trots in carrying a hand
blood spots a clean floor
knife falls out of tuxedo pants
a young man smiles and smiles
the world is so not what we say
sometimes so terribly not

cleanup

the small boy sat in the porch swing
rocked his body back and forth
to make it swing slowly
his eyes looked far away or nowhere at all
a policewoman stood nearby
a detective came out of the house
studied the boy who seemed not to see him
the detective knelt by the swing
the boy shifted his eyes to look at him
"can you tell me what happened?"
"I already did, you don't listen
he hurt my mommy, hurt her again
when she started to cry, I ran for her gun
I came back and shot him
he stopped hurting her
but it was too late
she won't talk to me"
the detective nodded and stood
"damn I wish he'd tell some other story"
the policewoman glanced at him
then went back to watching the boy
swinging again

Love in Interesting Times

love in interesting times 1

I always smiled at the Chinese curse
at least that's how I learned it
I suppose a different point of view
might find it a benediction
"may you live in interesting times"
who'd want to live in boring?
well, most of us some of the time
would surrender some of the "interesting"
for a little quiet, a little calm
a little bit of time to plan
as if planning had any chance
when tomorrow knocks the game board over
and soldiers order folks to dance
or cops decide a rally riots
or your boss sells your job and retires
or a meteor chances close to earth
or neighbor clears his magazine
by shooting randomly from his backyard
or boys nearby pick a girl to teach
them what sex is and love is not
or someone's dogs get loose and maul
whoever happens to walk by
and the world celebrates a random day
by shaking loose what we thought fixed
and maybe, maybe, just maybe
our job is not to walk the dotted line
and surely not to walk the plank

but to give each other space to breathe,
to dance, to curse, or build a house
to find another and grant that one
being the center of your world
no matter what the earthquake brings
maybe, just maybe our job's no curse
but "may you love in interesting times"

this girl

there was this guy, see?
and he had this girl
and oh, she was a honey!
and he was a jerk, see?
I mean, he made me look couth
except to this girl, of course
who thought he maybe set the sun
and brought it up again
he was her rooster
and I wasn't even her crow
and a smarter, suaver me
would've just let her go
moved on to another honey
who could see I had good points too
even if I didn't
set and rouse the sun
but luck's a strange dame
and I was there when he died
some kid he pushed around
one time too often
put a bullet through sun man's brain
right in front of this girl
and I was there to hold her while she cried
and suddenly a not-even-crow
became a little more
she ain't real sure she likes me much
but we've put the moon to bed now several times
and if she ever lets old sun man go
maybe I'll still be there

Valentine's Day poem 1 (for women)

I was thinkin', the tall girl said
that men are handy sometimes
whenever I want sex, for instance
it's never hard to find it
I was thinkin', the short girl said
that men are handy sometimes
whenever I can't reach a shelf
I need only look helpless
I was thinkin', the medium girl said
that men are handy sometimes
for makin' out or partner dancin'
or stavin' off the cold
I was thinkin', the old woman said
that he made most of my life mad
yet now I sometimes miss him so
he must've been good for somethin'

Valentine's Day poem 2 (for men)

I never knew how much I loved you, girl
til you went off to explore the world
and suddenly everywhere I looked
was where you weren't
every sound I heard was not your voice
every scent that teased came not from you
yeah, girl, you tied my world in a not
not you, not you, not you, not you
how could I not have known
you were the colors of the day
you were the sounds that prowl the night
you were the scents made breath worthwhile
you were the zests made my life sing
til you went off to explore the world
I never knew how much I loved you, girl

serenity

it isn't just the rain
that masks away the world
you come to bed
and worries, fears, and thoughts depart
they know they can (and will) return
but for these moments have no power over
comfort and grace and love

where are you when I need you

a young woman sat down on the same bus bench
which meant there was only a foot between us
except for the mile or so her look set there
the time for the next bus came and went
so did the next, "goddammit," she said tiredly
"there's a bar a block away," I sympathized
she looked at me again, maybe half the mile dissolved
"I'm not cheap," she defended
"thought you could use a drink," I placated
"all I offered," she disdained
I sighed and so did she, then we walked to the bar
what she ordered the bartender didn't know
so she told him how to build it
and she was right, it wasn't cheap
I sipped my Irish whiskey and admired
her steadfast attack on that strange drink
and when she finished, her eyes swam up to mine
"oh damn," she said, "I won't be takin' any bus tonight"
and so I walked her home and made us coffee
and stayed with her til both eyes worked together
"goddam," she complained, "ever' time I try to get away
another guy like you shows up, where are you when I need you?"
I found a blanket and covered her, "g'night," she said
and I slipped out, an hour later the bus finally showed

sleep well

rain drums on the roof
passing tires spray in counterpoint
drainpipe gurgles and
raindrops spatter from leaf to leaf
they make the hush that cradles sleep
so lover does not hear mate weep
they blanket the soft noises
of dressing, packing, leaving
til rain stops and a sunbeam startles
and man wakes to a half-empty
bed, closet, and heart
and wonders that he never heard it coming
as much as that he slept through her leaving
rain resumes, hush blankets early morning
but not the cry that celebrates her note
"Sleep well"

wedding

it was a wedding, yes it was
the bride was beautiful, yes she was
and the groom was, well, he was
he would have done better if he hadn't
goggled the bridesmaids, one two, three
or if he'd worshiped the bride more convincingly
like the best man did, unfortunately
and we'd've felt more comfortable, I'm sure
if the mothers has disguised their ire a bit more
and the preacher had known his lines by heart
but still the formal posturing all got done
and the magic words were said for all to hear
and the bride and groom left together at the end
and whatever else happened stayed off the record
so it was a wedding, yes it was
and we wish them the best, we do, we do

James and Jim

James and Jim were so close
neighbors laughed and called them brothers
despite their being born a month apart
in Marfa and in Taos
they played and fought together
a tag team in wrestling
infielders in baseball
and drinking buddies when no law prevented
until Janetta kissed James but would not kiss Jim
and laughed
and Jim spent three days reminding himself it didn't matter
Tara would kiss him and so would Emma and Leal
but always his memory burned with her "of course not" and her laugh
and one night walking home he passed her house
"good evening, Jim" she called and smiled
taunted, he decided
and in a fit of anger broke her neck
then ran
appalled at what he'd done
James found him
and they fought
so well-matched younger boys still talk about it
but Jim died
and James waits death in prison
whether by state or nature
and people whisper about friendship gone bad
or Cain and Abel
or that they somehow shared

a blood we don't
where did they find that blood some wonder

goddam

"goddam, I'm tired," she said as she sat down
she shrugged, "and not what you think
four hours walking, three men"
she grinned at me, "fucking waste
wouldn't you say?" I grinned back
"I don't suppose you have twenty-five dollars"
I did, I gave it to her, she looked surprised
"what you want me to do, and where?
you got a place nearby? cain't hardly do it
in the streets, not safe" she grinned again
"talk" I said, she laughed a burst of scorn
"talk? last man who wanted talk was my father
maybe my priest, not all they wanted
each was gonna save me, but save me too, y'know?"
I nodded, too familiar with statistics
"talk," she said, "you gonna listen?"
I nodded, she studied me then talked
told me how goddam much work it took
to barely make enough, never any to spare
"saw a movie once, y'know, 'Pretty Woman'
goddam, why couldn't that happen to me?
not once in too many years, not even close"
I told her it was a Cinderella story
"yeah," she said, "well, all I ever got was cinders"
she grinned again, "cinders and sinners"
I wished I could give her more, even if only money
but only had seven dollars left and needed that
"oh jesus," she said, "fuck, y'know?"
she grinned tiredly at me, a car drove up

she stood, walked to it and got in
the man slapped her and glared at me
they drove away and a bus stopped for me

postpartum

I forgive you for the moment
and if you knew what childbirth entails
you might appreciate that
interim forgiveness now
the baby is beautiful
even if he does have your ears
I hope he grows up to listen anyway
I hope he grows up with your courage
but not your fickle heart
I hope he grows up with your laugh
but not your willingness to laugh away my pain
he has your frown, I hope he grows up
without your willingness to scowl at my hurt
as if that would scare it away
he has your mouth, and like your eyes
it seeks my breasts if I'm around
or someone else's if I'm not
I hope he hasn't your brain
so I can teach him thought-piranhas
to gobble up any idea of an affair
or explanation that it was only while
I was too pregnant and wouldn't mind
y'know, I take it back
I unforgive you after all
if you don't pack and leave before we're out
the boy and I'll go somewhere else
somewhere thought-piranhas can flourish

conversation

what can we say now?
they caught us sitting on her front porch
well after midnight, sitting and talking
as if the night had shut the rest of the world out
and opened for us a treasure chest
whose every item needed to be celebrated
examined, and wondered about
so engaged in our new treasures
that we looked up smiling
as the headlight beam swept across us
and the car pulled into the driveway
she smiled and said, "my parents," proudly
as if she expected them to admire with us
no, they see no treasures, only two children
defying them and all people with good sense
and under their barrage jewels turn baubles
shatter and crumble, the chest splinters
she stands and flees inside
and her mother tells me in case I hadn't noticed
it's later than time for me to go
the next day she doesn't see me
and not because she's distracted
she looks away, suddenly intrigued
by her girlfriend's conversation
and treasure-dust is swept aside

reasoning

it happened one too many times
it couldn't be him
not that many times in a row
it must be her, it had to be
and so he walked out of the room
found his gun and walked back in
"honey!" she sympathized, he shot her
and up it sprang, ready as ever
there that proved it, didn't it?
it wasn't him, it had to have been her

wanted

"what do you want?" she said
"that's easy," he smiled, "you"
"hunh," she said, "not good enough
once you've had me you'll turn
to Carolyn, and Alice, Juanita,
Yvonne, and Mary Beth
no, if that's all, we're done
we've gone too far and not far enough"
"Wait," he said, "wait, not fair
you know I don't think this way
not naturally, but let me try
yes, I think so, yes, try this
I want a love my brother will envy
my mother doubt, and my sister scorn
'this is all her doing, you know
you couldn't make this happen'
yes, and I want it all with you
is that better?" he looked so proud
she studied him, puzzled
"goddam, I want to believe that
but it's so clear you said that
just to impress me, or yourself"
"No! No!" he cried, "it's also true!
try it and let me prove it to you"
she studied him some more and shrugged
"well, hell, even if you fake it for a while
what a love to live into! let's!"

endgame

how did it get this terminal?
one day at a time, I suppose
one argument allowed to stop
without resolution or apology
one huff carried away unsoothed
one flirt unresponded to
no one of them ended the game
but each like a diamond or a sword
added to a dragon's hoard
until the dragon grew too rich
and kind words couldn't best him
knight forfeits princess
and pawn takes knight
and board holds only useless pieces
all in bad positions
time for a farewell toast and wishes
followed by nights of whiskey

tell her

"tell her," he said and squinted at me
"oh gods, you don't know her"
he closed his eyes and breathed a bit
"tell her anyway," he said or cried
"oh gods, but what? I still don't know"
he looked at me, puzzled and still
"tell her I had no words, not for what
she wanted to hear, whatever that was
tell her I knew them for what hands held,
tongue tasted, eyes saw, ears heard, and nose scented
tell her...heart tried every sense for a metaphor
and still could not say, still could not say
not even now" he looked me his pain
then sighed and looked rested
I closed his eyes, sat with him a while
til paramedics and cops helped me let go
of his hand, of his arm, but not of his words

for a once friend

last beam from the quarter-moon
you said you felt as if you were
half-smiled and climbed onto the train
off to somewhere back east
Louisiana I suspect but do not know
a sinkhole opened in Lake Pontchartrain
and you never returned
although a not-so-friend
claimed he saw you in Kansas City
wracked out on drugs and disappointment
and talking to yourself
I remember you talking, laughing, teasing
until whatever happened and your eyes died
while your body kept on living
I remember we danced and I felt alone
and wondered if you did, alone in my arms
I stood there on the platform
and the train carried away
the last beam from the quarter moon

love in interesting times 2

we live in interesting times, my dear
the republic still shines
but it may be the glow
of death approaching
like those gay, giddy times in Rome
when citizens traded liberties
for a semblance of security
a semblance of prosperity
that never reached below the class
who might produce senators
consuls and governors of provinces
then died by the dozens
in their internal wars
their republic for some few years
seemed to shine as never before
then it was gone into an empire
but you and I may stand aside and watch
we never mingled with the class
who fund our senators and governors
who own our corporations
whatever it is they do now
we can oppose as well as spiders
prevent our going where we please
with cobwebs, that is to say
whatever we might do
they might brush off
or barely notice as they pass
ah, sweet lady, but we can love and do
can dance and sing and drink cheap wine

love by corpse-light still is love
just don't look at the glow

Last Words

May you have enjoyed these. May they have evoked for you your own insights, smiles, jests, laughs, and appreciations. May they have shared with you a perspective askew from yours. May you feel enriched by them.

www.ingramcontent.com/pod-product-compliance
Ingram Content Group UK Ltd.
Pitfield, Milton Keynes, MK11 3LW, UK
UKHW040557210726
13854UKWH00007B/1282

9 781105 549458